Dedicated to my husband Dr. Scott A. Rodeo, my children Scott A. Rodeo, Jr, Sarah C. Rodeo, Caitlyn M. Rodeo, and Mark D. Rodeo for helping me have it all; my family: Jean Frissora, John O'Brien (Uncle OB!), Chris, Meg (my Goddaughter) and John O'Brien, Jr, Joseph R. Frissora, Jr. and his wife Alison, Anthony, John Michael, and Joseph R. Frissora III, John A. Frissora and his wife Jessica and children Camden (my Goddaughter), Celia, Max, and Capri, David Frissora and his wife Kelly, and their children Maddy, Jacob and Riley (my Goddaughter), Mrs. Joyce Titus Reed and her family, the Rodeo Family; my endoscopy, anesthesia and Weill Cornell NYPH colleagues and staff for support, Awilda Crespo, M.A., Sonia Orona, Sonia Aracena, M.A., Rea Remedios, Eric Medalla, RN, John Ibay, RN, Maria Silva, Dr. Michel Kaheleh, Dr. Charles Maltz, Dr. Rebekah Gross, Dr. Sonia Olsen, Dr. Augustine Choi, the Authors on Park Committee for constant stimulation: Kara Ivancich, Holly Hunt (of Halstead!), Edie Blair, Alexia Fernandez, Susan Fisher, Lea Carroll, Susan Wald, Dr. Susy Olden, Karen Tompkins, Liz Cook, Jane Klein, Claudia Baez, Margaret McLaughlin, Anna Gilhuley, Jane Hemenway, Marge Bloch; Ralph and Allison Worthington; The Remsenberg Community Church; Michael Fontaine, Ph.D, Professor of Classics Cornell University, Rev. Herron Keyon Gaston, Yale Divinity School, and Laura Samponaro, Ph.D., Professor of Classics, New York University, for praise & encouragement; Michael Pecnik & the Viennese Opera Ball Committee, Alison Chase Brown for enthusiastic reading skills, DJ Pierce, Yu Kaneko, Tara Tunney, Ginny Pope, Caroline Rowley, George Yannopoulos, Traci Scott Karo, Linda Livanos, Josiah Eberhart, Susan Zeigler, Dr. Joe Sebeo, Gabriella Celi for joy & mirth,

Dr. Alisa Thorne, Jane Power & Laurie Leabu for endless and varied consults, the St. Bernard's Faculty & Coaches especially Alex Russell, North Landesman, Anne Nordeman & Mr. John Demeny, the true Prince; Maureen Burgess, Ph.D and the Hewitt Faculty, Alan Sash for power of conviction; the entire and extended Turner Family, the Johnson-Reilly Family, the Kelly Family, the Pulley Family, the Vogel Family & the Moran Family for endless, Allison and Ralph Worthington, Spiros and Antonia Milonas for gracious hospitality, to Joan Blacker Levine for endless creative energy and generosity, the Church of the Atonement for serenity, Margaret Hedberg & The International Debutante Ball Committee for elegance and grace, Theresa Fontana & Verna Merkel for friendship, Juana Libedinsky & The El Medano Club for vibrance, Voices Carry NY for mad fun, Professor Lauren Whitehead of Juilliard for excellence, Tennis pros of QFC and RC, James Harrison & Polo de Paris, and The River Club. To Sally Jennings & my tennis partners, coaches & opponents (without whom there would be less poetry, less drama, less life). To all who have supported me – and you are many.

In honor and in loving and enduring memory of my parents Mr. and Mrs. Joseph R. Frissora who gave me everything they could.

Introduction

March 2017

Dearest Friends and Readers,

"Christine, I didn't know you are a poet!", our (fabulous) tennis pro Jenny said when I read her the poem "Winning". It was part of a project I completed for Juilliard. It began, when I was going through a tennis tournament and a poetry course at the same time. My pro would say "hit it like you don't care" "don't be afraid" but of course my poems were full of anxiety because I had never really played in tournaments. At the same time, my poetry Professor, Lauren Whitehead, said "I want you to write these poems from a completely confident point of view". So part of these poems never really happened, some of them are invented from things I saw or heard, and some are written completely to boost my courage. Most people who read my poems, or hear me read them, feel they are there – inside the poem. When a fairly famous Latin Professor told me *he* "didn't know I was a poet", I had to confess I wasn't sure until that moment that I was.

The poems come to me in solid pieces. Another gifted classicist told me, "It's lucky you can do that – it's rare. You have to get your poetry out there –"it's just as vivid as what I read published." When my nurses heard "A Great Win" about saving a man on the tennis court, they said, "that gave me chills", and "I actually felt my hand on his chest too". My husband thought "What I Love About Him" was impressive and my little Mark after reading his poem said, "wow mom that's depressing!" It was written when he decided he was too old for me to cuddle. Still, after he read it, Mark was little nicer to me. That is the fun and joy of creating these short stories in prose. I have always been an avid reader – and particularly love Jane Austen and the classics. I learned to write by reading the best authors – Scott Fitzgerald, Ernest Hemingway, the Bronte sisters. I hate to be so bland but that is the truth.

Although I had never written poetry before, I seem to have a gift for capturing the essence of an experience. I can slice words. I can pretend to be Ernest Hemingway. I dramatize, exaggerate, reinvent, recreate, represent, misrepresent, distort and even lie in my poems – and no one knows! I always wanted to publish a book and every poem is it's own story. Learning about 100 literary devices – some of which date back to ancient Latin times which my son Scott Jr (a Latin major at Cornell) found for me, has been fascinating.

I want my children to have something of me to pass on to their children, "see this was my Mom. She was a Doctor but she was really a great writer." I also include some of their work, and poems we wrote growing up, as part of a family memoir. Apparently, every great poet writes about the same 4 or 5 topics over and over. I didn't know that when I began. I only knew that people said my poems convey emotion and my words have power "that's exactly how it felt", "that's exactly what it was like – you captured the experience perfectly". If you like my poems it's because you see yourself in them. If I am lucky, you feel yourself in them.

The rules to creating a good poem seem simple. Write about what you know. Think about what you are trying to convey or what emotion you want to evoke. Strip the poem down to only essential words. Get rid of every extra word. Hemingway did this - chopping down the sentence to the bare minimum. Choose the best word. Stack images on top of each other in layers that the reader can feel, see, and smell. Try to impart a feeling or emotion. Describe how you felt, not what was said. Describe a sensation to someone who may never have felt it. Rewrite the poem 3 times. Poetry does not have to rhyme. There are 100 literary devices. Play with them. Hemingway said to always mention the weather – but it's up to you!

Writers have to experience life to some degree to write about it. My themes are my family, tennis, heartbreaks of various kinds and I leave you to find the fourth! The connection of poetry to tennis may not be obvious at first - but every tennis player talks about "getting in someone's head". There are so many factors (audience distractions, noise level, white noise) that affect performance during a match. I use poetry as imagery to visualize and mentally rehearse my matches. I am only a beginning writer and a beginning champion. Let's talk again in a few years when I have more to say and have learned more to share. It's a journey for now. Welcome aboard.

Christine L. Frissora, MD, FACG, FACP

"Dr. Christine Frissora, author of Beyond Onomatopoeia, shares an extraordinary brilliant collection of inspirational poems that is provocatively transformational. Her pearls of wisdom on these pages will provide you spiritual nourishment and encourage you to tap into your own creative genius. Her work is passionate, fierce, challenging, inspiring, and engaging. If you are interested in claiming your inner strength, making your dreams a reality, and pushing yourself to achieve greater heights, then this book is absolutely for you!"- Rev. Herron K. Gaston, Yale University Divinity School

"These poems should be published and be out there since they are so beautiful and vivid"- Laura Samponaro, PhD, Classics, New York University

"With this collection, the Doctor has found her muse! Her deeply personal voice takes us on one journey after another into the triumphs and foibles of daily life." - Michael Fontaine, Ph.D., Professor of Classics, Cornell University

I begin with the most recent poem I wrote that actually inspired me to finally publish this book. This is a class by itself because I never wrote about an animal before.

This is my floater – a sample of my style and sets the mood for the book. I hope you enjoy it. I hope you see him. It is about a horse I saw when I was playing in a tennis tournament in Uruguay. Most poets write about 4 things over and over – I write about my family, tennis and heartbreak. I don't know why!

Arabian

Clear blue sky dry wind rolling hills
crest of deeper darker lustrous blue beyond
where the hills meet the horizon
we trod plod calmly easily readily happily willingly
stop at an invisible wire fence
see him prancing
his head large body compact
neck ripped with muscles
at an angle like an accordion
sun kissed copper freely flying over the prairie
hoofs are up he dances flaunts
muscle youth power strength joy freedom everywhere
He sees me watching him
breathless stunned stilled watching seeing absorbing memorizing
the most beautiful animal ever seen
not an animal a stallion
He is the Arabian, she says
I stare at him he glances at me
I stare at him he turns away leaving
coyly he glances back
eyes at me
one last look as he leaves
my heart breaks just a little
and I think he did it on purpose
the next day there is something small fast and yellow green
high flying over to my right
I turn a bit cross leap reach strike
free effortless volley smash
a beauty they laugh
I think of Arabian

Here is one about Medicine and Tennis - perhaps the most important poem I have written because it will save lives, is true, and teaches what to do in an emergency. The basic thing is to get the defibrillator on the patient as soon as you can- the machine will analyze the rhythm for you and may talk to you as well. Call 911. Breathe for the patient if you have to. Learn the basics through The American Heart Association. Here it is! The following is published in the Ascensus Journal of the Humanities, Weill Cornell Medical College 2017.

Caption: I have always been an avid reader. A few years ago, I was struck by Ernest Hemingway's biography and read a book about how he wrote. He cut words. Sliced everything down to the most bare meaning. Chose the single best word. The fewest words. Said to include the weather whenever you could. It is sometimes hard to read – it is prose. Last year I took a course at Juilliard with Professor Lauren Whitehead, "Poetry and Performance". At the time, I was going through a tennis tournament – a novice – but my partner was strong and if I kept the ball in play we got the point. We made it all the way to the finals of the Bs. Still, I was fraught with anxiety, being the weaker player. I started writing poems full of imagery – slice the ball, cut the ball, close the point. Choose the best shot – the same way Hemingway chose the best words and cut the unnecessary. Still the poems were full worry and Professor said, "Rewrite this from a totally confident point of view". Not easy when you are at net and they are ripping the balls at your chest (knowing you are the weaker of the 2!). Three sets and 2 tie breakers later we lost the finals by 3 points but our pro Paul let us move up to the As because we fought valiantly! So here I am, a year later, with Alexia subbing in for her friend and having mad fun. I am going back to the office for 1 o'clock fellows' GI clinic at Weil Cornell when the pro comes to us at check out "Call 911"! The rest… is history. *Dedicated to Alexia Fernandez who could have played with anyone.*

A Great Win

It was just a day
a beautiful day
because I was going to play tennis
with my friend Alexia
Nicky couldn't play she needed a sub
I see her
Alexia is there already
Green cat eyes smile
We play we laugh we run we win
We lose we laugh more WHAT?!!!
The girls leave they have to take the tram at noon
I don't leave - I have my car
It won't save any time for them to drive
but Pedro will hit with me for 10 minutes
I am sweating
Pedro it's great! you go to your next lesson
I'll pick these balls up
then, "Christine- do you want to play with us?!"
Do I want to play with us?
I look over - one pro and 2 guys
they need a fourth
Ilovetoplay
OK thanks! but only for 10 minutes
I have patients at 1
We hit I volley we laugh we win
I have to go
"We are both Henry's easy to remember" the guys laugh
I wave goodbye
"I hope we can play again"
I check out pay my bill
Sign up for tennis team

"Call 911!" It's Pedro
Is someone hurt? I am a doctor
There's a man down?
Get me the paddles
Let's go to court one

I see him

Lying still a gash to his right temple bleeding
an agonal breath
He fell?
He has a heart valve- he is on coumadin
the men standing around him say
there might be a thready pulse
"He is breathless" I say
Lift the chin and head back
I breathe into him
There is gravel and blood on his face in his eye
I lift the shirt place my hand over his heart
still no heart beat
the paddles are coming
a few more breaths
he is cold clammy still staring into space
Unresponsive I have lost him
An agonal breath?
Did he breathe?
The paddles are small stickers
they are on the chest
Back up green button analyzing
CLEAR

Shock

,

6

I breathe into him
Heartbeat under my hand is strong now! Fast!
The breaths are agonal
I assist him
Pedro brings me the oxygen
It is cranked up and I mask him

I breathe into his chest and he keeps breathing

I keep my hand on his heart
I feel his life tenuously in my hands
if I stop breathing he will die
Strong beat. Perfect.
Take the pads off
I don't want him shocked accidentally
He gets stronger he fights me
"Henry! I am a doctor breathe slowly don't move!"
He is agitated now moving everything
He is strong!
He was dead now he is strong!
EMS arrives
He fell - he has a valve on Coumadin
I breathed into his chest and he breathed
No Epi but he is agitated
"Yeah, that's what happens when you bring them back"
I am so happy relieved surprised

My knees are cut my lip is swollen and bruised
I walk to the locker room

that's when they see me covered with gravel and blood

all over my beautiful white tennis outfit
the girls in the locker room offer me soap and a towel

they are so impressed but my knees are bruised and scraped
"I never did that before"
I am beat up exhausted
I go home I shower I clean my
mouth where I cut my lip
on my own tooth
Scrape off the gravel and dried blood
I go to the ER
He is awake alert talking!
His EKG is normal

He is perfect

There is a hush of excited admiration
among the doctors
I am happy so happy so grateful so glad
I am at peace
I call my son and tell him the whole story and now
He wants to be a Doctor
I am happy so happy so grateful so glad

I am at peace

Comments by the reviewer: Wow- What an amazing story, and I love how it unfolds in the poem so unexpectedly and so vividly! Thanks for sending- will pass along. L

FAMILY SECTION – mine, theirs and ours.

In order of importance: my family poems are first. My husband read *Katerina* about our little girl then (young lady now) and asked with a grin, "Who is the strongest man in the world?" There can be no doubt, Caitlyn adores her father. Always questioning why the other Dads aren't as strong, and fit and handsome as hers! Scott was a Stanford swimmer so that is tough to compare "average" Dads to. She will understand someday! So here is Katerina followed by a poem I had to write for my husband.

Katerina

pure clear naiive simple
graceful delicate ready to be crushed by the world
if not for the love of the strongest
man in the world who molded
an iron butterfly

perfectly formed cut
light like every morning spring
and every light lithe flitting flowing being
living art is she

gentle happy during every
curve of the run
at once small capable efficient reliable

at once ethereal distant contained

she is not cool
she is more than cool
more than anyone

he never liked cool girls
that run in packs
he said no one likes them
She is little wife and lets no one near him

She is Caitlyn

My husband loves my poetry writing. He is a gifted, very focused surgeon - but somehow he gets me, gets the poetry, gets the whole thing. He always notices when I allude to him in a poem (see Katerina!) so I dedicated an entire poem to him this time. I do my best writing at the River Club after tennis, in the Via after my Juilliard Class, or at home when the children are asleep. Usually the poem hits me in a conglomeration of words and sentences. Somehow by the end, a clever title with a double innuendo pops into my mind. There it is. It just takes 2 seconds. The key is having something passionate to write about. It is nice to have instant feedback on poems and here is from Scott & my sister.

What I Love About Him

He doesn't have Facebook
He likes my singing
He thinks my poetry is impressive
He thinks I should be a pianist
He reads Nature
He earns a lot of money
He spends none
He doesn't care about tennis but rips the ball effortlessly
He uses my face shot as his screen saver
He is cut
He doesn't wear a ring and he still
doesn't sleep with other women
He always says I am
the prettiest girl in the room by far
and means it
That is why I love my husband

Note to readers: Scott loved this. I think you should try to write to your loved ones – even if you are not the best writer.

. . .

From: "Rodeo, Scott MD" <RodeoS@HSS.EDU>
Date: October 18, 2016 at 4:31:02 AM EDT
To: Dr CFR <frissoramd@aol.com>
Subject: New Poem

Wow.
You are awesome!
I love you.

On to Mark - a charismatic little guy who can break your heart when you aren't watching!

Mark

cool soft luscious white skin
a pillow under my lips
clear bell voice
into my soul
light bright quick funny witted little man
pure joy to snuggle against
when it is
code
breathe his life into me
and be still
it is over now
little man looks straight through me
will not be cuddled
is not a baby
will not come to me
will not call for me
not *even* when he is cold
states the little man
I cry inside
implausible
next time I will shed tears
maybe
he will change his mind

Mark D. Rodeo, Age 12

Our son Scott is a Swimming Champion, President of the Cornell Triathlon Team and just placed 3rd at West Point.

Scott is a gifted Latinist, a fine musician and a kind, pure soul. Scott did the same thing Mark did but he was only 6!!!!

Scott

eyes clear blue round crystal balls of marble
skin smooth but deeper than that
the gentle soul of ocean
an abyss a haven where I flee
and bury everything into him
at peace
quiet calm unending
I have never been loved so completely
so perfectly simply
until
"You go"
the wide eyes
firm face
jaw fixed
He is clear he is certain
I am to leave
I do not know what to say
so I just leave
and wonder

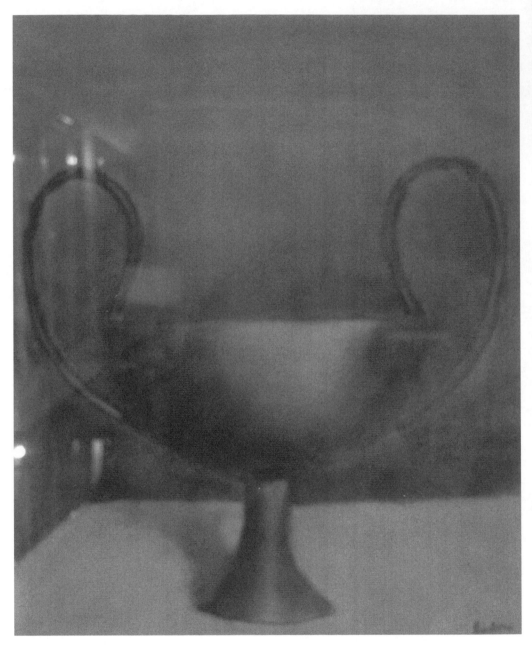

Scott A. Rodeo, Jr, Age 11

Our Sarah is a Vassar student and scholar of many things. She was just accepted to the Yale Divinity School and Institute of Sacred Music. We are thrilled!

She is an Organist and an engaging Choir Director for St. James Church in Hyde Park, among her many other accomplishments. Sarah has become one of the most fine young ladies anyone has known. Board members who meet her at Vassar, where she is a Music liaison, ask to meet me. Sarah is special. Many people could change the world. Sarah will. She is so special and we all look forward to seeing great things from Sarah.

Sarah Rodeo, Age 11

Tiny Princess Young Woman

Delicate well formed
perfectly formed tiny delicate hands now
that used to be thrown over her head as she slept
like an exhausted little princess
skin clear peaches eyes crystal green
something delicate porcelain intangible
unspoken present felt sensed shared underneath
gentleness now grace intellect refined
open always open mind spirit heart
ethereal untouched unspoiled endless promise
laughing at post it notes from decades ago
mirth happiness so much to come
A lovely young woman

This is a nursery rhyme - we made "Caty Cat" up on the way from Oia to Thira in Santorini. My husband, my 11 year old daughter and I were walking along the most beautiful stark blue gray black and white path but it was hilly steep and hot for her at times. Her mood cycled with the steepness. So we said this alternating echoing and over and over until I thought my husband was going to kill me! **"OK I get it about the bloody cat!"** You say it in a syncopated way – the rhythm is like the Adams Family theme song.

Caty Cat

I had a cat
a beautiful cat
a tiny cat
a beautiful tiny cat
an exquisite cat
I had a cat
a beautiful tiny exquisite little Cat
I had a cat
a Caty cat
a beautiful tiny exquisite
little
cat

I had a cat ….

& repeat!

At 10 Gracie is a little poem by Caitlyn (age 11 at the time). She wrote it in Ithaca when we were visiting my son Scott at Cornell; we stayed at La Tourelle.

She wrote this while I wrote Third Set Heart Breaker.

At 10 Gracie

You enter a marble built palace
Princes greet you kindly
Willingly assisting you by helping to carry your luggage
They park your carriage efficiently
You take a step into a magic box which takes you up to your home on a magic carpet
Then you know you have reached your final destination in peace

When Scott Jr and Sarah were little we had a huge 1100 outdoor terrace in New York, by the hospital. We had a comfortable swing we called the "rocky rocky" and on that swing I would rock and sing this to them (Sarah notated it in 3 minutes!). A song is prose put to music so here you are!

It starts off "Rocky, rocky rock you're my little rocky rock rocky rocky rock you're my little rock rock rock."

Dedicated To: My First Set of Twins, Scott Jr. & Sarah Rodeo
I Love Them, Love Them, Love Them!

Lyricist: Dr. Christine Frissora   Composer: Dr. Christine Frissora

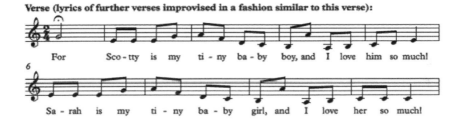

My family gets my poetry - maybe because they lived it or know me so well.

I hope my readers get it. On November 3 something exciting happened to me but I didn't know until November 4 - my brilliant college Vassar girl daughter commissioned a poem from ME. My first commission!

The poem came to me after tennis, when I was in a VIA. I wrote it from 52 second street to 69th street.

Unlike most poems, I did not rewrite it once. It is there - complete and imperfect. Of course this opens a whole new category of writing for me: commissions!!!

It went like this:

On Nov 3, 2016, at 11:37 PM, Sarah Rodeo <sarodeo@vassar.edu> wrote:

Hello Mother!
My friends have some poetry commissions for you!
Will you write us a poem about bad church music?

Beautiful Bad

Grates on the soul
Brings you down
Every genre of music
Has good beautiful and bad choices
Except this
This is all
Bad
Where there was elation hope joy
Is now a sinking twisting angry
Feeling in my left side
No soul to sing
No desire
It has brought me down
When you sing you pray three times
But this is no song
No prayer
This is nonsense
Complete utter nonsense
Waste of time when life is
So short
Where are the crossing harmonies
discordant tones juxtaposed like a tight fence off balance
Where is beauty peace harmony
So many choices and they give us
Nonsense
I can't even sing it
I won't sing it
Boring repetitive simple dull nonsense
then I hear it
Behind me the voice of an angel
A sound so beautiful

He can make THIS sound like that?
Heaven soul God is here
Ok I'll sing it
I'll sing it like THAT
I hear it now
Mimic copy breathe sound listen
Joy now
Anything can be beautiful

———-Original Message———-
From: Sarah Rodeo <sarodeo@vassar.edu
Genius we love it. We will have more commissions for you later

REALLY?!!!!!!!!!

For posterity another child's poem

Sarah's first poem Age 5

The Car

Wheels rolling,
engine running,
what a famous car.
We watch them glide
on the streets of Nyde
and watch them roll along.

Mark's poem he wrote for St. Bernard's – "found poetry" as though it was a note he left (for his father) on the kitchen counter.

Sorry Dad

My pants are on the floor
Right where I left them
By the sink

My sneakers are safely stored
Under the round ottoman
Perfectly hidden from human view
Right where I left them

Yes, that's my milk on the counter
Right where I left it

The wet towel?
Yeah, it's right there
Thrown on the bathroom floor in a puddle of water
Right where I left it

My room's not a mess
I just like to see everything at once
all spread out on the floor

Oh! Were all the lights on AGAIN?
Yeah, that's just how I left them

Sorry Dad!

Love and War

Reluctantly he comes into my room
It is late he is tired
He has showered brushed
I have trimmed all 20 nails
Cleaned the bites with peroxide
His skin is soft
in this last minute of boyhood
I can't find the baby powder
I am slightly disappointed
he jumps onto the bed
In his state of exhaustion
and maybe deep down contentment
he puts his head on a pillow on my lap
let's me play with his hair
I have waited all week for this
It has taken every bit of cajoling to get here
I am so happy
I begin reading to him about the bunnies
the brave one, the one who tricked the eel with clay, the bunny with bent
ears, the little bunnies that are tharn
He listens relaxes
I get him for an hour of timeless peace
He sleeps
There is something he wants from me
an expensive lacrosse stick
In the morning before church I get to read to him again
he reads too
he likes these bunnies begins to understand who they are
the challenges they face
I take his sister to choir practice
We read a bit more when I return

but he is at his limit
has had enough
bolts to his room locks the door
I go down to the canal to check the lawn for geese
We have just repaired the invisible fence with sticks and branches
checking now for leaks
I am serene calm happy walking across the lawn
his reading voice and the sufferings of the bunnies still in my head blue
sky green grass clear wind
ONE GOOSE
Maybe more?
Mark help me!
the geese are here!
I grab a tennis racquet
a lacrosse stick a shoe
On the attack
but it truly is only 1 goose
I throw a few things to get it to leave my grass
the dumb thing challenges me rather than leaves nicely
Wings up hissing ready to jump on me
I threaten it into the plastic fence
It cannot escape and the neck is caught
Bloody bird!!!
I hear my son dismayed exclaim "MOM!"
Like I meant to hurt it
I just wanted it to leave
Now I have to release the damn thing
I walk gingerly to the plastic fence and free the big bird without getting
bitten
It is in shock
It is fine
It jumps into the canal swims away
It studies me carefully before it goes
I stare at it imprinting my face on the brain

of that bloody bird so it never comes near me again
I scream at it to get out stay away from me
I hate geese
I gather my weapons
The tennis racquet the lacrosse stick the shoe
I put them away and walk upstairs to wash my hands
Were you surprised Mark?
Yeah
Surprised that I captured it or that I let it go?
Actually, Mom- both

Title _____

Author _____

What are you trying to convey _____

Cue _____

_____
_____
_____
_____
_____
_____
_____
_____
_____
_____
_____
_____
_____
_____
_____
_____
_____
_____
_____
_____
_____
_____
_____
_____
_____
_____
_____
_____
_____
_____
_____
_____

Title _____
Author _____
What are you trying to convey _____
Cue _____

_____
_____
_____
_____
_____
_____
_____
_____
_____
_____
_____
_____
_____
_____
_____
_____
_____
_____
_____
_____
_____
_____
_____
_____
_____
_____
_____
_____

Mark D. Rodeo, Age 11

SECTION II: TENNIS

I started my first Poetry course when I was in a tournament with Alexia. We got to the finals by luck and inches. We lost the final (B) by inches – see Third Set Heart Breaker.

A topper is a favorite line; a cue is focusing on what we try to convey; and the goal in this one was to write from a confident point of view. A year later, with much more experience, I don't think about a lot of it anymore but when I read these poems I am shocked by their detail and the imagery really does help to prepare for a match. Even now I get lost in them. I submitted some of them to Sports Illustrated and they said, "we don't publish Poetry" and I replied "YET. You don't publish poetry... yet". Poetry or prose is such a natural way to prepare – people do it in their own minds without even realizing. That is why in tennis they always say "she got in your head". Stay in your own head. Who cares about them? Play the ball. Move forward. Hit hard. Bottom up. Have fun! Remember a lot of this is contrived and may never have happened – it is a conglomeration of a lot of matches I saw, heard, or experienced.

topper: We keep breathing in and exhaling power .....
cue: clear up the cast of characters; who are we
goal: write it from a totally confident point of view

Winning

We are a new team and they do not know us
we do not yet know ourselves
they all see us moving up the ladder in the tournament
fairly easily - so far we have not sweat

We are the gracious queens that rule the court
stronger together than our separate sums a natural synergistic team
we are surprised
we feel our power and so do they
our power together overwhelms them

There are moments of clarity on the court when she looks at me
as if to say that was a good one or
no worries here we are stronger take your time
keep it in play slow the ball down
she loves my down the line so I do it again
she praises my low in the middle approach shot
I do it over and over
she laughs and tosses her head
I do not know what she is saying
but I like the sound it

Like the Women's US swim team filming Call Me
before they conquered the world
we are laughing and loose
we are fluid and soft
we are naïve, charismatic and effervescent but underneath the charade

We show our true metal when we have to
we play just hard enough
we watch and wait

we do not make the same mistake twice
Let them make the mistake

We play our game and so do they
I am loud "you missed it" "that was out!"
We do not like that line call and let them know
We are way ahead
Do.not.break just put it in play

Placement over power
Keep the pressure on
Hit it like you don't care
Pretend the score is 0 - 0 don't do anything different
Hit it hard enough not too hard
Squeeze the racquet handle before you hit
Don't move until she hits
Remember the lob - just lob if you are in trouble
Mix it up - hard and soft - down the alley and in the middle
Finish the stroke
Step forward keep moving forward
Run to the net it throws them off
End with your racquet up

For a moment my partner cannot return a serve
I look her right in the eye
Just be you - you are good enough
Don't do anything - just hit it back
Move your feet, bend your knees; bounce and hit; follow through
my partner laughs she finds it amusing when I yell at her
but the next balls are in and the game is ours

She says it was an honor to play with me
I frame the letter
her words are more important than the win
but the win was nice

About the Game

It was never about the game
Love life friendship
Power.
Maybe winning laughing running sweating praying planning
Practicing drilling
Wishing hoping
Ok
Maybe it was about the game

Cue: why did I write this poem: because I broke in the third set and will never do it ever again

Prompt: describe *how* it felt not what they said

Dedicated to: All who have helped in innumerable ways - you know who you are

Third Set Heart Breaker

White noise buzz air thick on court
first point in play is ours
She, fluid free effervescent smiling
My right hand

First game serving opponent aced
next a tiny flick of the right wrist inward
a love game ours
AMAZING gleam her green cat eyes into my left chest

BACK UP PLAY BACK she commands
it is time to be smart not brave
we run in together power from behind
a comet forehand smash from the right hand
sweeps the ball off the court
opponents disjoint confuse discombobulate
no retaliation yet
the set is ours

Focus. forget incessant ignored foot faults
Block. children running Block. disloyalty injustice ignorance
Block. rudeness Block. conceit Block. arrogance anger bias prejudice
Block. everything

There is only us the yellow ball and this moment keep it in play

We struggle, touch everything
moments of brilliance moments of gripping ugliness
moments of everything no moments
volley smash hit opponent at net
Apologize.

Third set opponent cannot serve
hits her partner in the back
they disintegrate fall part cannot return a ball
momentum on our side
BLOCK it.
We are up 4-1 it feels effortless surreal we are thrown

Suddenly insidiously impossibly there is no yellow ball
plans evaporate tactics dissolve there is no court no space lines fade
no right hand no left
We. Break.

The longest tennis match in our history is at end
We generated excitement hope interest joy
We worked practiced planned played prayed performed the best we could
Never gave up fought until the end.
Novices against captains

We lost the match but Won our Game

Thank you

A Hard Lesson

560 balls she says
a wicked kind smile and lilt in her voice
focus on the spin
spirits high I head to the baseline
bucket after bucket
feel the rhythm
hit it in front
aim 3 feet over the net
swing through step forward
that gets the ball deeper
I feel it memorize it copy it replicate it freeze it in my brain
75 of them in the alley down the line
Switch
Back hand cross courts she stops
Where did this come from?
I am left handed comfortable here I control the court from here
See? I lob over the net person like this
They run for the back hand
but my partner smashes it
Or I go down the line like that
B.A.S.H.
Or the down the middle approach
See?
She is amazed stunned stilled quiet surprised frozen stuck baffled
she cannot feed a ball for 30 seconds
I am delighted thrilled ectastic
I watch her brain turn it over
I see her seeing us winning crystal
Spell broken
I have to make this HARDER for you
Inside out past the service line

15 in a row
Now she is training a champion
Fun over
It's time to PLAY

feedback from the pro Gabriella: What a beautiful morning read to wake up to! I LOVE it!

I have spoken to many women over the months that I have been playing in tournaments. They all tell me they feel attacked when their partner is stronger than they are. "All the balls come to me!" That happens in mixed doubles when the male is strong because people are afraid if they give the ball to the him it will be ripped back - irretrievable. Still there are some men that are all over the court stealing every single ball making it impossible for the woman to even hit one. The Court Bully hogs every ball and bashes it at the female opponent. This is always unnecessary because the bully could place the ball anywhere, and not physically endanger anyone. Still it happens enough that I include the poem here.

Court Bully

He is big she is small
her balls are angular
I need more on my legs more on my lob
more more more
hit is faster
it's a big serve
hit it faster
swing earlier
I hit it straight up to the sky
he misses
stand there
in front of me
more to your left
the bully at net is jamming everything at me
my serve my add
I want this game
He looks at me puzzled
OK I serve I return
he volleys
point game
We are all laughing
I want to try it again
he feels we won't be lucky the next time
he resists me and I don't have the energy to discuss tactics
I can't get it away from the bully
I need to go higher
but that bully is everywhere
Hogging every ball
Jamming it at me all the time
When my partner touches a ball he rips it
The bully won't give him another chance

It's all me now
I return some not all balls
the balls are a little too fast for me to see them
Don't see them just use your reflexes
opponent's husband
"Oh WOW a male pro bashing a female member"
but I am stronger now
I can't lie
I want to play back
Partner is stuck in the middle
We have to play smarter
there is not time to plan
Another time
Another day
I will lob higher and make him play
Australian

Flash

unintentional mishap
wardrobe misfunction
oh no! look at this
ugh not THIS so sorry
grin laugh
well now we're *really* partners
balls on fire
ripping down the alley
opponent can't see them
a slight brief struggle
then we are free clear
it is butter effortless
some concentration
everything is in
opponent watches the ball rip down the alley
too fast to reach for
opponent rushes prematurely to net
my perfect high lob over her
ball drops dead short well in
ignored untouched
luck power skill laughter
easy win
WOW all that from one flash?

Doug & Max- thank you for today! This covers both lessons. Now if I just Remember to do it! I promised Max I would put him in a poem so here he is immortalized! I am cc Gaby because she knows I am going into a new tournament.

Final Lesson before the Final

Air sun wind laughter
Skies bright clear crystal blue
boys laughing on the court
I want to play too
OK he grins
split step and drive it
You're against the wind here
Lob it higher
Better on defense but where is my volley?
A kind smirk
Maybe it's your foot work
totally definitely right
time for my own lesson
Let's go to court 7
It's all about foot work
See? Hit it right there
Keep the body turned
Follow through above your shoulder
Keep the ball on your racquet
Long slow strokes
Stand here move forward at an angle
Turn and bend your knees on the low volley
Wide stance keep wrist firm
One simple slanted movement
Chop
Punch the volley away
Use the corners
Watch the ball until it leaves your racquet
Follow the volley into the alley
Not too much
It's all about moving

If you move well you'll play well
Hah then I'll keep moving so at least I look good
He smiles. YEP!

The Match

She is strong gentle calm laughing
I am free
We pull the net across the court
Our private battlefield
We serve laugh hit
We are playing
the ball looks beautiful
A simple yellow arc over the net
Back and forth
Somewhere we are conscious that we are beautiful too
The girls are mesmerized
We are fun to watch
So we play for them
We entertain them and each other
Insidiously they fade disappear
Depart
My energy does too
I have to concentrate more
Oh just have fun!
Fun? Kiss of death for me
A sudden glimpse of the girl with the big smile
I hit a few more
She leaves I fade again
It's more fun with people watching
I miss I laugh don't care
Why didn't you lob me?
You didn't even try on that one!
I did try
Just not hard enough

2 things.
I miss you, I love this.

—

gabriela celi

producer | sound post, film & tv • fitness events
tennis & fitness instructor | • private training

Dr Christine Rodeo <frissoramd@aol.com> Date: 08/19/2016 8:09 PM
(GMT-05:00)
Subject: The Match (draft 2 - every poem has to be written 3 times)
Do you like this better

The Match

She is strong gentle calm laughing
I am free
We pull the net across the court
Our private battlefield
We serve laugh hit
We are playing
the ball looks beautiful
A simple yellow arc over the net
Back and forth
The sky looks beautiful
The air clear
Somewhere we are conscious that we are beautiful too
The girls are mesmerized
We are fun to watch
So we play for them
We entertain them and each other
Insidiously they fade disappear
Depart

My energy does too
I have to concentrate more
Oh just have fun!
Fun? Kiss of death for me
A sudden glimpse of the girl with the big smile
I hit a few more good ones for her
She leaves I fade again
It's more fun with people watching
I am playing a deer
I watch her run back and forth never tiring
She is fun to watch
I am listless feet heavy slow lazy
I miss I laugh don't care
Why didn't you lob me?
You didn't even try on that one!
I did try
Just not hard enough

To: Alison Chace <alisonchace@aol.com>
Subject: Re: The Match (draft 2 - every poem has to be written 3 times)

The first one feels more poignant

To readers - was it more poignant because she read it first? or was the first draft "better"? Next time you pick up this book, read Draft 2 first! Email me your feedback!

This was written after hitting at the River Club. Fernando Martinez hit with me and my husband as a favor to his dear friend and Golf buddy Kenneth Laub.

My husband started on Fernando's side of the court. Later, Ken couldn't resist the fun and despite a having bad hip, he jumped on the court, on my right.

Fernando at the River

Eyes bright blue he seemed happy to play
Stepping onto the court
Ok let's hit some
Can you take feedback?
Wrist firm
Catch it like a baseball
No flick
No extra movement
Simple clean motion
Left foot to the side
Stay open
Same thing on the backhand
The left hand leads
Good!
Too much fun
Torn hip man can no longer resist
takes 1/2 my court
Let him play with my husband
They are intently quietly having fun
but still in my way
How much information can you absorb?
Good!
Stand 2/3 between the net and service line
No closer
That's your place
Watch the plane
Do not move forward if it does not cross the plane see? Recover
Again firm recover
Backhand recover
Concentrate focus
High low recover recover

Low volley ugh again again again
Hands closer together on the racquet
They should touch
Jump! Jump HIGHER
You can jump you have to jump
Overhead off the back foot
Now the front foot More!
Overhead. Put it away.
That's good
You had me worried for a minute
Stand further to the right
You left too much of the court open
Stop! get ready before the ball bounces
Don't run in like an Indian
Let me see the serve
The power comes from the core
From the lats let's put more on it
Get ready get ready
recover recover recover
Smash the overhead
The torn hip laughs exclaims shouts
Delighted thrilled relieved surprised
EXCELLENT !

My friend Cynthia Foster invited me to a tournament in Lyford. It was very special and I got stronger. I made friends with Nora Holmes and joined her tennis team! That may have lead to saving a life (*A Great Win*).

Lyford Magic

Life after the hurricane she writes
Trees or no trees we are safe
The tournament is to be played
My husband urges me to go
You will have fun
I am at the airport 2 hours before boarding
Implausible I am never early
No good doctor is ever early
Implausible I woke up at 7
It's just after 8
Implausible
I.have.nothing.to.do
Spa relax
Really?
How long is a pedicure and facial?
I have time
I have time?!
excitement is too much
I choose my color my chair my French tips for 10 extra
I chill I relax
the pedicurist Diligently perfectly takes 10 years off my feet
I noticed that!
my partner would say later
When did you have time to do that?
When did I have time to do that?
I was early for my flight
I met the nicest girls
Well someone was quietly siting next to me
It looked like a foot massage
In walks big smile girl
I can't believe this!

I am taking a picture of this!
I see the racquets
Two of them or 3
She breaks strings?
She must be good
They are laughing
Are you playing at Lyford?
Yes!!!! Did Cynthia invite you?
YES!!! She invited EVERYBODY
Blonde girl works at Tiffany
She can sell nothing
Trump protestors block her doors
You sell silver on the third floor?
I NEED the silver disc for gifts
We can do it on the phone!
Well you should play USTA
Really?
It's fun you can be on my team
Really?
Do you want to see me play first?
No.
I read Wonder on the plane
Jack deserves the prize
What a strong special adorable boy
I tell my son he reminds me of Jack
He hasn't read it
I'll give it to him at Christmas
Nassau is sparkling clean
I see no hurricane trauma
No one was hurt
Thank God
They all grin at me
Can I have that smile?
Do I seem happy?

Blonde girl just asked me to play on her team
She is a 4.0
of course I am happy
The taxi is 20 cash
Hello Mr Gibson I haven't seen you in a while!
The gate keeper smiles
We arrive at Lyford
Pink orange green happy heaven
The air feels happy
I am going to play
My partner warms me up
match starts
we fight to the end
Such an ugly win
We'll pay for it tomorrow
but for now it feels so good
Blonde girl is at our match
We are not drinking
Big Matches tomorrow
We sleep well
That was smart she says
We both play we both lose
We drink wine with big smile girl
At cottage 104
pink blue happy the guys joke
they are sitting across from us to admire the view
Blonde girl laughs
I am in sweaty tennis whites
"For everyone that says it 50 think it"
we laugh it must be her blonde hair
she decorated this in 4 weeks?
Yes and the mark up from palm beach was 50 per cent
There are no matches for me tomorrow
I will go home early to help my husband

"You have to learn to chill"
my partner instructs
I had a pedicure!!!!!
They want me to be happy
Brunette college girl
who volleys like she is 16
hits with me
We sweat!!! I made her sweat!
Blonde and big smile girls
Play with me
I am so happy
I have a drink ticket still
I send emails to all the girls
"Doubles anyone?! Bribe: a shot of rum punch. I am by the pool"
Now I am sitting by the pool
Hoping someone wants a shot of rum punch
Aperol
Then I will get them to play with me!

I wrote this for the nice guys that have played mixed doubles with us this summer. We have a few ladies and these guys jump in and rip everything - it is mad fun. The ladies in these games remembered these moments, loved the poem & feel the same. It is a combination of the guys in our summer games and my husband. The guys know which lines apply to them but any lady playing mixed doubles with strong players knows the thrill of it. Why doesn't it hurt when the guys hit us? We just laugh. Getting hit in ladies doubles is a way different experience. Maybe because it doesn't come with a heartfelt apology, ice and lots of attention.

Feel free to use this to thank your mixed partners. We are stronger - thank you for playing with us

Why We Like It

We like to play with him
He makes us
laugh run smile jump forget
grow stronger
He yells that's SO HOT
when we rip it past him
We like that all 27 courts hear him say it
We do it again
We like when the guys on the next court break into laughter when
they see us rip it right into him with all our might
We like when he laughs too
We like when he rubs our shoulder blades to loosen our serve
We like it more when he stops because he knows it hurts
We like when we move on purpose and he misses
We like watching him transform into a machine set by set
We like that he is strongest when the other guys are tired
We like that the moment he steps on the court there is more there
He steps into the ball arching it deep to the base line
We like stealing his power with our volley

We like it when we make such a good shot the next court claps
We like that he smiles too
He is beautiful to watch when he serves
we forget to watch the ball
We like when he asks if he is serving too hard
We like when sets up games for us
We like that he walks over to book the best court at dawn for us
even though he isn't playing
We like to laugh run smile forget grow stronger
We like that he likes to play with us

About Our Match

I am excited
I am playing with Lisa
This is going to be a fun one
We are going to win

I watch her in warm up
Lisa has gifts
a ripper beautiful forehand
that should set me up for life

We start
Lisa rips I pounce volley score
First 12 points ours without a heartbeat
No resistance. Nothing.
We are cutting through butter
THIS.IS.FUN!!!!!
THINKING 6-1 6-1
MISTAKE
NEVER THINK THAT

At changeover opponents start the bullshit
You are a great team! Have you played together before?
No we never met
We smile though. We are a great team.
We feel the power. Click click click no problems
They are going down.

They compliment Lisa on her strokes, her game
She deserves it - she's a beauty.
Somehow they get stronger
we get weaker

I lob I short shot I put more spin
Lisa goes down the line wins her serve
rips that forehand so low I don't know how it comes back
but the bloody ball comes back!

I lob and lob
they make a few mistakes
Every point now a struggle
luck on their side
They hit the tape. We miss it
I rip my backhand we win the game
but I am ripping too late
I am behind the curve
I play back one point - ours
We are playing against a wall now
Where is the butter?
I can't do enough I can't set her up
tonight I am not enough
it is not my court

We lose 4-6 3-6

next time?
IGNORE opponents
HIT HARDER FASTER DEEPER EARLIER
NEVER BREAK
PUT MORE ON THE LEGS MORE ON THE BALL MORE SPIN
MORE MORE MORE
DO NOT THINK IT IS EASY
NEVER. GIVE. UP.

WIN!

Tennis Under the Green Grey Water

I have just bought a wet suit
have never owned a wet suit before
never worn one
I am on the beach
ready for the practice course
I don't have my medical wristband yet
I walk forward chin up shoulders back
past the security check point
no eye contact
I am not yet an Ironman
I am trying to look like one
I am going in that water
I am in
I have not checked the course well
a knife of ice water
goes down my back
inside the suit
I am awake now
I am doing my best freestyle
pretending to be real
almost crash into the dock
I don't yet know the secret about looking straight
head above water before
turning my head to breathe
He will show that to me later
my goggles are foggy leaking
Is there such a thing as a perfect goggle swim
No pressure no leak no fog?
ignore it. block it.
Look under the water
I remember something about

buoys on the left rope on the right going out
now I see no markers
the lake is mine
No one is doing a long
course the day before I can't see much
Where are the buoys?
I have to go around an island alone
I could go under no one would ever know
I am 1/2 mile out
no rafts or humans in sight
completely unsupported
If I stop swimming I will die
the thought thrills me
I keep swimming I am not tired
water is green gray blue sky is blue grey raining
I glide through the water in that suit
there's a reason people wear these things
Have I ever been so relaxed free calm alone
He told me I will burn a ton of calories I will shrink
Will I?
I swim to the next buoy
I am thinking now of another boy
who has just promised to play doubles
an hour after his flight lands from Asia
What is he filming in Asia?
In return I have promised him a poem
to be read at twilight in front of our friends
on the tennis court between sets
sipping seltzer water preferably berry
preferably cold
preferably with hot pink lipstick on the edges
in a dream ice and pretty glasses
I see the scene clearly
We are grouped around the net at the side

The park is green quiet sunny it is dusk
I am at buoy 6
can only see my hands under that misty water
My hands and feet are numb
The rest warm in my skin tight black and pink igloo
In my mind I am choosing
the right words the best words
I can't speak talk write
I am under water
I have to memorize them
He has special traits
Everyone wants to be his partner
He makes the court happy warm exciting
He laughs rips runs laughs
His boyish charm is contagious
Destroys your back if your serve is tight
You and I are the same person
He explains on the court
He speaks in simile
We have to just rip everything
Don't be afraid of a mistake
He does not yet see that my rip against them is not enough
I am not enough
I am not strong enough I can be smarter
I am consistent they feel me there
they know I am always ready for the next ball
I can run but not backwards
because my knee comes out
He likes to play with me
I can lob it right over them
to the back hand
He can have the set up the overhead
he can take the kill
I just need a minute

just give me a minute
3 balls see the space
feel the pace spin it
Place it be patient back up a bit
Wait
smash at the right time
Play a little further back
Brace yourself in case they rip it at you
There isn't enough on my serve
if I can just get 30 per cent more on it
Spin it follow through with the wrist
There! to the back hand
he is set up for the volley smash from his forehand
the ad court is a different play
I spin it low annoying obnoxious to his backhand
Watch the alley just in case
He misses we laugh
Stand at the service line until my shoulder is loose
Want me to loosen it?
That's a hard decision
Yes and No
He smiles he knows it hurts
Assess my serve from the service line
go forward or back with every ball
Split step before they hit
Stay to my left
Stay within 12 feet
We are connected by a string
Let's move up together
It freaks them out
We have a plan
We are a wall
They are not
Do you see this invisible wall right here? Do you feel it?

A pane of ice right here I mime a wall -
if the ball is in front of our wall we volley
Place it don't waste it
Follow the ball
Split step
It may take 2 or 3 volleys
There is no rush
Do you get it?
I am talking to him
but the other one watches listens takes it all in
Don't talk during a point
Don't think so much
Just play!
We need to learn to play well to train well from
the beginning
We play how we practice
Choose the best shot now
so when we are under pressure we do the right thing
Pretend this matters
Winning is a skill
We have to practice winning
They are my champions
My heir my spare
I have chosen them they have chosen me
I need them both
can't miss a match can't miss a tournament
need the adrenaline to survive
crave the rush
We will tap their strength
power rigor vigor youth vim to win
They are smart they listen they trust me
They question me but they begin to see
We play more matches we get stronger
We are all learning together

We will go to nationals if we work together
If we pull our strengths attack their weaknesses
Isolate the weak opponent
Take the stronger one out of the game
Aim for his left shoulder I say over and over
See those pink sneakers?
That's your target memorize it
I am at buoy 10 I am turning around
I can't see anymore markers
I am a mile out
How long have I been in the water?
We will go to nationals because we will
and next summer
I will be an Ironman

Title _____

Author _____

What are you trying to convey _____

Cue _____

_____
_____
_____
_____
_____
_____
_____
_____
_____
_____
_____
_____
_____
_____
_____
_____
_____
_____
_____
_____
_____
_____
_____
_____
_____
_____
_____
_____
_____
_____
_____
_____
_____

Title _____

Author _____

What are you trying to convey _____

Cue _____

_____
_____
_____
_____
_____
_____
_____
_____
_____
_____
_____
_____
_____
_____
_____
_____
_____
_____
_____
_____
_____
_____
_____
_____
_____
_____
_____
_____
_____
_____
_____
_____
_____

SECTION III: HEARTBREAK

I am writing this section with my nieces and daughters in mind – having just had long walks and talks with these lovely young women as they decide how to face the rest of their lives.

Love is only Fun if it's Rough

Who said that? Who sang that? Why do girls feel that way? Anyway, for all of us who fell in love with bad boys in high school or college or maybe later at work, before we met our Prince - take heart. There is a good guy out there for you. If someone is unappreciative or mean or neglectful walk away right away. There are a million people who would appreciate you. Go find one (or two!). Most of these heart breaks poem are about men - other things can break your heart of course, but it's usually men. Notes on syntax: you can use capitals, or not, grammar or not, periods or not. It's your poem - write it in a way the conveys your meaning in the best way. It never has to rhyme, although repeating words, sounds, rhythms can be effective.

Rarely does a poem take me 5 drafts to get it perfect - and maybe the first draft is better anyway?

𝓕ake 𝓞ut (draft1)

She loved easily readily quickly
heart open ready waiting
He elated excited flattered
desiring attracted fell in
quickly easily readily
almost drowned
Jumped out of the pool
Readily quickly easily
and ran

𝓕ake 𝓞ut (draft 5)

She loved easily readily quickly
Heart open ready waiting
He elated excited flattered
Desiring attracted fell in quickly easily readily
Almost drowned
Jumped out of the pool
Readily quickly easily
impossibly implausibly rudely cruely
left her to drown
and ran away

Title _____

Author _____

What are you trying to convey _____

Cue _____

_____

_____

_____

_____

_____

_____

_____

_____

_____

_____

_____

_____

_____

_____

_____

_____

_____

_____

_____

_____

_____

_____

_____

_____

_____

_____

_____

_____

_____

_____

_____

_____

_____

_____

List of Rules Poems

Cue: who you are to self; what everyone else says; stack images
Note: Whatever your profession is – substitute it when I say Doctor. If you are a male just reverse the sexes

Necessary Advice to Smart Young Women

First, do no harm. Unless someone tries to harm you or your family. Then go after them in every possible way and employ every tactic in your arsenal. Now is the time to be relentless. There are 100 ways to hurt someone. Use them all and think of new ones. Be gentle on yourself. Focus on the positive. Walk with your feet. Appear stable at all times. A Doctor must appear stable at all times. People will think you are unstable if you are always acting unstable. Do not allow anyone to make you feel less than you are. People are jealous of everything. Call the lines fairly, but honestly. If a ball is 99 per cent out it's in. Do not give them 2 inches, unless you are way ahead and the game doesn't matter. Then you can be generous and smile, 'that's too close to call - great shot'. Say, 'brilliant', when you are losing. Support your partner. Say 'good idea' and smile no matter how stupid the shot was. If he looks at you like that, stare him in the face and tell him he is too old for you. Tell him you prefer men with more hair or more money. Do not drink in public ever. It will lead you to apologizing for things no one ever knew you did. Read to your children. Make them read to you. Pretend you like it. Teach them how to use 6 pieces of silver properly. Teach them not to be easily impressed – or at least not to admit they are easily impressed. Don't buy them iphones. Do not buy cheezits either. They go to your thighs. Do not swear in front of patients or children. It kills angels. Do not swear on the tennis court. Throw the racquet if you must. Never be late for endoscopy. If you are, apologize and buy lunch. Say kind things whenever possible. People repeat what you say. If you want to vent, vent to someone who is out of the loop. Be sure they will never be in the loop before you confide in them. Only put things in the email you want to share with the world. When someone says, "be careful what you put in email – it can get out there", pretend to be shocked. Be as wise as a serpent and gentle as a dove. Try to laugh when you can. Try to laugh last.

Spoken & Un

Words spoken
Anyone would love to have you under their roof
I didn't remember your eyes were so blue
You and me?
Wow That's exciting
They are lucky to have you
Pic
You
G nite baby doll
You're very desirable
very attractive
His words are drugs
Even now they cut sear burn
She shouldn't remember them
But she does
They are branded into her left chest
To recall is mostly agony
Only moments of bliss
In a sea of misery
I'm going to choose my words carefully
I need you to hear these words
Okay?
her heart tearing shredding burning hurting
Maybe earlier...maybe later
but not now- now is not a good time for me
Seeing you would be 180 degrees opposite of what I am trying to do
right now
I'm sorry
Disappointment anger disdain disbelief shock
I shouldn't have done that
I will always love you

Words unspoken
You didn't come earlier
You can't hold me to that
You can say anything
face to face
She still believed
he could not say no
If he saw her face
What's that baby doll
She wanting waiting craving desiring
He not
He is only cherry poison
His words are drugs
He is poison
Heaven poison and Hell
Mixed in cherry syrup

A Small Figure

A slight blonde, a small figure
happily following her friend home after school
trotting along as always
happy and bouncing, then sitting on the porch, waiting for her friend.

The air was still and quiet and she was serene,
happy and content to wait for her friend
to play hopscotch and jump rope
to relish in a few hours of calm after school.

She was good at school
she had beautiful clothes that were always edged with exquisite lace
and impeccably pressed.
She had the most beautiful clothes of anyone she knew
because her mother worked at a dry cleaners.

Her father worked in a factory
even during the depression they worked.
On Fridays Daddy made a traditional dish of white rice, tomatoes and onion,
the tomatoes were from the garden behind their house
Daddy spent hours in the garden, behind the house
there were green beans and grapes, tomatoes and so many things in that
small place of earth

She did not know they were poor

She had a sister and she had an uncle
There was always someone living in the house
her mother, who worked at the dry cleaner helped them
her father, who worked in the factory helped them too
All through the depression they both worked

They bought Grandma a new red coat
because her husband only married her to work on the farm
but Grandma loved the farm

all of this existed in her independence, strength and a dogged ambition

but the poverty

the poverty she was not aware of pervaded everything
she was not yet aware of it sitting on the porch and waiting for her friend
for a few hours of peace and playing hopscotch.

The door opened
she looked up with the blue eyes, white skin and blonde hair, and tiny
perfect frame
and saw a large man come onto the porch where she was waiting for her
friend.

"You don't belong here" he said, in a firm voice
"Get along home now"

Those words, spoken for a myriad of unknown reasons
cut through the soft heart of the gentle girl
the gentle girl that would never hurt a soul
the lovely girl with every possible god given gift that she could never see
because the stigma of poverty burned her

She did not know how to verbalize the shock, sadness and surprise
She did not know where to bury the disappointment
The heartless words buried into her soul
She remembered them for her entire life

and that ignorant man I could kill with my bare hands

Girls Die

Girls can
Die of a broken heart
die of happiness
die of delight grief shock shame
die of joy
Die of anything really
Men
Men don't die of anything
They live free going out
They never have to die
of anything

They just leave

Moonlight

A pretty girl in the moonlight
laughing drinking daring playing trusting
simply perfectly carved white marble skin
in the shade against the black rock above the gorge
White silk marble
curvy smooth soft toned perfect now
Flaunting beauty youth power to the night to the angels Heaven
God me to herself
prancing holding kissing touching
a woman child in my arms now gazing up into my face
the sweetest voice intently explaining what I don't understand
I listen
I still don't understand
Does she?
She is somewhere else
Craving something else
Missing something else
Wanting something else
time passes quickly easily happily
She just wants to play
She wants to play with me
She is safe here so she plays
I watch her
She is rapturous manipulative captivating innocent as a child guilty
as sin
She makes it as hard as she can
Against my will I touch her
it feels like Heaven
so soft smooth round silky with baby powder
She will tell me later that her princess hair can cover her chest
I will ask her to prove it

She stacks images purposely
She is remembering a moment about a wine glass
I am lost
I touch her skin below quickly lightly
I am dismayed surprised not surprised not dismayed
I forget any simple touch imprints on her forever
Forget her memory
Forget the power of my words with this one
Forget each weapon arrow thoughtlessly insensibly fired
into the heart of the angel voice pretty girl
with the soft supple thin body of a virgin
Who is mine no more
left cut wounded harmed angry wrathful gone
She does not forgive me for what I do not apologize
She cannot forgive me for making her bleed for leaving her bleeding
alone
I was unprepared
I did not mean to make the soul of an angel bleed

Title _____
Author _____
What are you trying to convey _____
Cue _____

_____
_____
_____
_____
_____
_____
_____
_____
_____
_____
_____
_____
_____
_____
_____
_____
_____
_____
_____
_____
_____
_____
_____
_____
_____
_____
_____
_____
_____
_____
_____
_____
_____
_____

SECTION IV

A short section. Things I don't like: pests of all kinds!

I was debating including this one but one of my faculty advisors felt it was honest and should be included. Then my daughter sent me a safety advisory! In it goes!

From: Kim Squillace <kisquillace@vassar.edu>
Date: April 17, 2017 at 9:44:07 AM EDT
To: "all@vassar.edu" <all@vassar.edu>, "students@vassar.edu" <students@vassar.edu>, emeriti@vassar.edu
Subject: [Students] Campus Advisory

Please be advised that the Canadian geese are now nesting. They are located on our property at the farm and sunset lake. Please keep a respectful distance from them as they have recently been reported as aggressive. Should you have an encounter with the geese, please let us know.

—

Kim Squillace
Associate Director of Safety and Security
Vassar College

. . .

From: Gaston, Herron [mailto:herron.gaston@yale.edu]
Sent: Friday, April 14, 2017 5:32 AM
To: Christine L. Frissora
Subject: Re: thoughts on this one?

I think it reads as an honest assessment of an authentic experience you may have had.

Invaders of Two Kinds

I hate geese
They were on my lawn
I asked them to leave
They did not
I screamed they moved
Goose stuck in plastic by neck
I would have left it
I thought it dead
Worker across canal comes to my lawn
Get off my property
I came to help you
I will get scissors
Who are you?
It's suffering
It is not suffering it is still
I will release it
If I need you. I will get you.
You need to leave.
Goose is gone.
He is on my property!
You could go to jail for that
They are wildlife
I thought she was dead
I would release her
You have to get off my property
You are not allowed on my property
Prat. Pests.
Both. Gone.
Me chasing the geese across my lawn
I would have left it as a warning to all geese.
Had it not been for the prat.

Title _____

Author _____

What are you trying to convey _____

Cue _____

_____

_____

_____

_____

_____

_____

_____

_____

_____

_____

_____

_____

_____

_____

_____

_____

_____

_____

_____

_____

_____

_____

_____

_____

_____

_____

_____

_____

_____

_____

_____

_____

_____

_____

LITERARY DEVICES

Bear in mind that poems have no rules, that each poem is it's own piece of art and stands alone; and there are over 100 literary devices you can use. Chances are you have them in your poems naturally already. Here is my top 10 list – ranging from common (stale), uncommon, and intriguing devices to consider in your work.

Onomatopoeia - the namesake of this book the word sounds like what is it "soft" "gurgling" "click"

Double Entendre - the first meaning in double entendre is usually straightforward while the second meaning is ironic, risqué or inappropriate

Allegory - "All animals are equal but some are more equal than others"

Alliteration - a number of words, having the same first consonant sound, occur close together in a series

Hyperbaton - similar to anastrophe, which is the inversion of the natural word order "some by virtue fall"

Non sequitur - Latin phrase that means "it doesn't follow" random, disjointed, incoherent thoughts

Stack images – layer it all in

Ellipsis - omit some parts of a sentence or event, giving the reader a chance to fill the gaps

Aphorism - a funny truth "Having nothing, nothing can he lose."(Henry VI)

Oxymoron - combination of two contradictory or opposite words "original copies" "thundering silence"

Dear Readers,

Thank you for finishing this book. A few sources I have enjoyed and found helpful:

Ernest Hemingway *On Writing*, Larry Phillips, 1999 – a pleasure a treat a thesis a masterpiece a must read

The Elements of Style, William Strunk 1918 – tedious, dense but so helpful and essential

The Writing of Fiction, Edith Wharton 1924 dry but probably helpful if you can get through it

Bird by Bird, Anne Lamott 1994 a fair source if you like her writing

My Absolute Must Book List

Ernest Hemingway suggested 20 books to read (see Larry Phillips book) some I have read and some I have not. After a lifetime of reading everything this is my short list. The books vary in age time and flavor but these books are all fascinating in their own way.

Jane Austen – everything

Bronte Sisters – everything

The Scarlet Pimpernell, Baroness Orczy 1905 - brilliant engaging

Laura Ingalls Wilder – everything - whether she wrote these books herself, or her daughter Rose helped her is unknown but they are beautiful stunners of early American life. *Little House in the Big Woods* (the first one) is tedious and was meant initially to be a "how to" book. Perhaps do not encourage your children to start with that one – or if she does skip the boring parts.

Ernest Hemingway – hard to read – chopped especially his short stories – prose but so worth it. Sadly died by suicide late in life as did his father.

Scott Fitzgerald – easier to read than Hemingway takes a minute to adapt but wonderful commentaries on life. It ended badly for Scott – his "beloved" Zelda was candied poisoned syrup and may have encouraged his alcohol for some unknown reasons. He died young.

A Wrinkle In Time, Madeleine L/Engle (Grade 6 and up – 5th graders really can't grasp this easily with pleasure)

The Chocolate Money, Ashley Prentice Norton – raw shocking bare brave (age late high school or college and up)

Those Who Save Us, Jenna Blum, 2004 – beautiful and real

Have fun practicing! You shall hear from me again in a few more years have I anything else fascinating to say. Please contact me with any feedback, questions, or concerns. I am available for poetry readings, library events, book clubs and luncheons and love to travel - especially to talk about writing and poetry. frissoramd@aol.com 646.209.5211

Title _____

Author _____

What are you trying to convey _____

Cue _____

_____
_____
_____
_____
_____
_____
_____
_____
_____
_____
_____
_____
_____
_____
_____
_____
_____
_____
_____
_____
_____
_____
_____
_____
_____
_____
_____
_____
_____
_____
_____
_____
_____
_____

Appendix
Featuring Caitlyn Rodeo

When you create your own poems and share them with your friends and family you may see an explosion of communication and energy. These poems were recently written by my daughter Caitlyn. She just turned 13. My son Scott and Sarah commented on them immediately and I feel she deserves her own appendix.

I AM PUTTING Caitlyn in an appendix in my book She is becoming a writer!

From: Caitlyn Rodeo [mailto:crodeo@hewittschool.org]
Sent: Wednesday, April 19, 2017 1:17 PM
To: Christine L. Frissora
Subject: Poetry
Hi mommy!
Here are some of my poems:

When Spring Comes
When Spring comes
Things will be different
Skies of grey will transform into pale blue
The naked trees will be abundant in fruits and leaves
Dry plains of grass will be a painting of vibrant green
Sand-like soil will be rich and nourished
The isolated sun will reveal its radiant beam to the Earth
Snow will be melted as gentle rain will water the white daisies
My whole entire family will prance with me in the beautiful field
But only when spring comes

I asked her to choose the best word and to take out unnecessary words

Caitlyn Rodeo age 11

When Spring comes

Things will be different
Skies of grey will transform into blue
Naked trees will be abundant in fruits and leaves
Dry plains of grass, a painting of vibrant green
Sand-like soil will be rich and nourished
The isolated sun will reveal its radiant beam to the Earth
Snow will melt as gentle rain will water the white daisies
My whole entire family will play with me in the beautiful field
But only when spring comes

The Vacant Field

I look up at the roaring cloudy sky above me
Observing the dead, bare trees
Feel the dry, grey soil beneath my filthy bare feet
Breathe in the chilly fresh air
Mountains stand in the far distance......
This field continues beyond my sight
Shelter is miles back
Though I stare straight ahead, in this
Vacant field

She cut words and selected best words for:

The Vacant Field

I look up at the roaring sky over me observing the dead, bare trees
Feel the dry soil beneath my filthy bare feet
Breathe in the chilly fresh air
Mountains stand in the far distance......
This field continues beyond my sight
Shelter is miles back
Though I stare straight ahead, in this
Vacant field

99

From: Scott Rodeo [mailto:sar266@cornell.edu]
Beautiful!! those are seriously good!! I love the imagery
From: Sarah Rodeo [sarah.rodeo@yale.edu

Amazing, Caitlyn!

Bye mommy! ☺

Title _____
Author _____
What are you trying to convey _____
Cue _____

_____
_____
_____
_____
_____
_____
_____
_____
_____
_____
_____
_____
_____
_____
_____
_____
_____
_____
_____
_____
_____
_____
_____
_____
_____
_____
_____
_____
_____